I
Can BE
ANYTHING
"Super Boys"

By Amber Ferguson

I
Can BE
ANYTHING
"Super Boys"

By Amber Ferguson

Dedicated

TO ALL THE DREAMERS

"You can BE anything. Follow your dreams."
-Amber Ferguson

All the things I wish someone would've told me as a child...

Amber Ferguson

Did you know?

You can be anything you want to BE!

So, what does that mean?

You can BE an Astronaut!

You can BE a Doctor!

You can BE
a Judge!

You can BE a News Anchor!

You can BE a
Business Owner!

You can BE an
Author!

You can BE a
Ballet Dancer!

You can BE an Athlete!

You can BE a Chef!

You can BE a
Pilot!

You can BE a
Dentist!

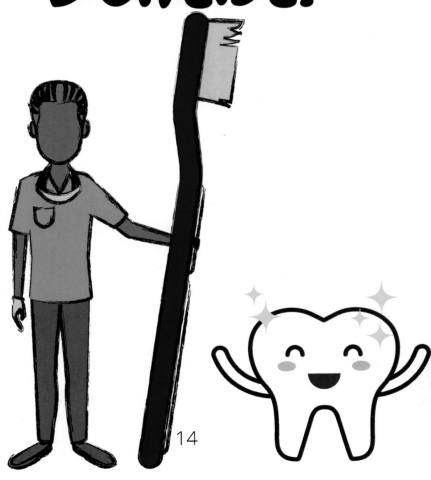

You can BE President of The United States!

You can BE a
Wonderful Father!

You can BE a Husband!

You can BE a Teacher!

You can BE a Race Car Driver!

You can BE a Social Media Influencer!

20

You could BE a Professional Diver!

You can BE an Architect!

You can BE a Clothing Designer!

You can BE a
Stock Broker!

You can BE a
Fireman

You could BE a
Real Estate Broker!

You could BE a
Scientist!

You could BE a Motivational Speaker!

28

You could BE a
College Graduate!

You could BE an International Spy!

You can BE a Movie Director!

You can be anything you want to BE
BUT
You have got to put in the work.
Nothing is going to be easy.

Some of us must work harder to prove
ourselves more than others. It's just
the world we live in.

Keep your head high little brown skin
boy; You can be anything. Endure.

You can be anything you want to BE.
The sky is the limit.

And guess what?
They say the sky is limitless.
So, that means you have limitless potential.

The World is waiting for you!

No one can do anything quite like you!

So believe in yourself.

Stay in school & study hard.

Don't let anything or anyone
put any doubts in your mind.

Hold tight to what you believe.

Trust your parents advice.
Let them be your guide.

When you feel like life is
too tough..
Remember those that
paved the way.
You have everything you
need within you to make it.

So go be a shining star!

Be Exactly Who You Are!

Shine bright for the World to see!

And go BE
Whoever,
Whatever,
and/or
Anything Else...

That You Want to BE!

What Do You Want to BE?

Don't worry if you're not 100% sure.

That's what growing up
and different experiences are for!

You're going to change your mind so many times!

But trust me,
one day, sooner or later ...

You'll know
exactly
what you
want to BE.

So make us proud!

Don't BE a Follower or Get lost in the Crowd...

You are meant for
great things
in this World.

Now go BE a
Super Boy!

Write Down What You Want to BE

Write Down What You Want to BE

Write Down What You Want to BE

Don't just talk about what you want to BE. Write down what you need to do to get there!

Don't just talk about what you want to BE. Write down what you need to do to get there!

Don't just talk about what you want to BE. Write down what you need to do to get there!

Write down anything on your mind here!

Write down anything on your mind here!

Write down anything on your mind here!

Who can help you reach your potential? Write these people down here:

Who can help you reach your potential? Write these people down here:

Who can help you reach your potential? Write these people down here:

A Space to Write What Ever You Like...

A Space to Write What Ever You Like...

A Space to Write What Ever You Like...

I want to know how far you go!
Keep me in mind as a behind the scenes
mentor. If you're under 18, Get a parent's
permission & you can keep me up to date on
how you're doing or let me know if you need
any ideas on what you can BE!

Email me at:
ceo_amberonie@plusmebrands.com

This book was written with intention to inspire, empower, educate, and encourage.

As a brown skin girl, I have had to persevere, show grit, and walk in my purpose with my head held high and most times; all by myself.

It is my hope that not one brown skin child ever has to feel this way. There should always be someone waiting to lift you and build you up.

You got this. You are not alone. You can BE anything.

Remember to **lift** someone up today.

Amber Ferguson

The next few pages are intentionally left blank.

Made in the USA
Columbia, SC
15 September 2022

67169067R00046